MY
BROTHERS'
KEEPER

Advance Praise for *My Brothers' Keeper*

"In this intensely intimate account, Gloria Reuben reveals how the deaths of her brothers led her to a deeper understanding of the importance of family bonds, spirituality, and ultimately the joy of being *My Brothers' Keeper*. Beautifully crafted, Reuben must confront the endless questions of 'why' and 'what ifs' after her brother David's death at age twenty-two. Years after the sudden death at age fifty-nine of her brother Denis, she finally finds peace, coming full circle in her quest, relishing in the joys that each shared and the life lessons she carries today as an actress and, more importantly, a loving sister, because of them. A read, at times sad, but an inspiring love letter and reminder to all of us who have lost siblings."

–Pete Earley

"Anyone who has lived through the death of a loved one should find comfort and truth in these pages."

–Jessie Close, Author of *Resilience: Two Sisters and a Story of Mental Illness*

MY BROTHERS' KEEPER

Two Brothers. Loved. And Lost.

Gloria Reuben

Post Hill
PRESS

A POST HILL PRESS BOOK
ISBN: 978-1-64293-410-6
ISBN (eBook): 978-1-64293-411-3

My Brothers' Keeper:
Two Brothers. Loved. And Lost.
© 2019 by Gloria Reuben
All Rights Reserved

Cover art by Cody Corcoran
Author photo by Aaron Sarles
Interior design and layout by Sarah Heneghan
All photos are from the author's personal collection.

Post Hill Press
New York • Nashville
posthillpress.com

Published in the United States of America

To all who seek solace
from the pain of losing a loved one
~brother, sister, parent, friend~
I hope this book helps bring you
peace of heart.
Hope for the future.
And a knowingness that you are not alone.

*Special thanks to David Vigliano.
Your belief in me and your unwavering
support right out of the gate will forever be
appreciated.*

Table of Contents

DAVID AINSWORTH REUBEN

JULY 28, 1966 – JULY 25, 1988

Chapter 1
The Visit

It was the magic hour—that slip of time when you're not quite awake and not quite asleep—on an early morning in May 1998. I was in my home on Westridge Road in Brentwood, California. I loved that home. It was a sweet, cozy place, perched on the side of a canyon, with a wall of glass generously offering up gorgeous views of the mountains cupping the valley. And on those rare days when the smog played hooky, a spectacular vista of the great Pacific waited.

I was dreaming of my brother David. I don't recall the details, but I know it was a dream about him, for I felt the restlessness in my body and the longing in my heart that I always felt while dreaming of him.

David's death, twelve years ago this year, has left my shattered heart still in shards. I try to piece it back together. Smooth out the edges. David was two years younger than me, and his death crushed me.

I feel like I failed him. Like I didn't take care of him as I should have, since I was the one who was closest to him in age. Since he and I were the "unwanted" ones. The two Reuben kids who were born after my father had prostate trouble. We "weren't supposed to be here."

A few days before his twenty-second birthday, David gave away the few possessions he had. Then he swallowed a bottle of antidepressants.

It's the most difficult thing, not being able to say goodbye. Wondering at least once a day what his last thoughts were that made him decide ending his life was better than continuing it. Recognizing every day in my own life, the loneliness and isolation that drew him to that choice. Drowning in the certainty that it's part genetics, and part unspoken and unhealed emotional and psychological distortions that enveloped our home while we were growing up.

The dream ended. I was semi-awake. Groggy. The sun must have been on the rise, because my bedroom held a natural glimmer of golden light.

He was there in the room with me. My brother David. I felt his presence as if he were standing right there in flesh and blood. His soul reached out to me, and he asked without speaking, "Do you want to see what it's like on the other side?"

I thought I was still dreaming. I could feel my spirit move towards him. I wanted to go. Join him. See what it was like. But then fear entered my heart. A distinct and strong feeling overcame me...I might not come back.

All grogginess dissipated. I was now fully awake. David was gone. Again.

If he asked me today, I would go with him. Even if it meant that I wouldn't come back. It would be worth it, just to be with him again.

July 2000

I was born the fifth of six children. David was the youngest. Jesus, he was a beautiful child. And I loved him. I still love him more than I can express.

I have no children. None of my siblings have children. Our perspective, our hope for bonding with others in a familial way, was marred from our debilitating upbringing. At least that's what happened with me. I actually shouldn't speak for anyone else (something I continue to learn quite late in life).

Yet before the time when even the prospect of having children existed—before David's death, before the death of my father when I was twelve—there were pockets of laughter, levity, and love.

I wish I could give you countless specifics or a detailed timeline of my first twelve years of life. Believe me, if I could, I would. But I can't give you what I don't have. And I don't have the memory of much of those years.

But I can capture and share with you the feelings, the snapshots, the beauty and joy of two siblings who spent a lot of time together.

David and me—maybe it was because of some instinctive yet unspoken knowingness that we were pocketed in a separate way (unexpected births), or maybe it was just the nature of things, but we were two peas in a pod.

We played together. Simple, fun stuff. Thank God it was a time long before cell phones, so our young eyes and minds were not glued to numbing and desensitizing screens. We were the lucky ones, being raised in an era when you could ride your bike for as long as you pleased, experiencing freedom and independence while winding through tree-lined streets and returning home as the sun started to set. Zooming toy Mattel cars through Lego-lined villages set up on the basement floor. Ice skating on the front lawn after an ice storm shuttered the schools for the day. Raking fallen leaves as autumn set in. Splashing to our hearts' content in the small wading pool in the back of our house when the summer heat bore down and we needed a little cool escape.

It's so sweet and sad, thinking of those innocent days.

Have you ever wondered where you would go or what you would do and say if you could travel back in time? I understand that it very well may be a futile and silly waste of time even thinking about it, and as a relatively intelligent person, I'm not proud of mentioning it. But I do think about it. I ponder it a lot.

If I could indeed time travel, I would go back to the age of six. David would be four. I would take his little hand and walk with him to the field that surrounded the elementary school we attended in Guildwood Village (in Scarborough, Ontario, a suburb of Toronto). We would run free and play. Laugh and roll on the grass. Gaze at the clouds, finding our favorite cartoon characters sketched throughout them.

Popsicles and peanut butter sandwiches would magically appear, and we would devour them with delight.

We would while away the day.

And as the sun began to dip, I would take his hand yet again and lead him home. He would be fed and bathed. And I would tuck him in, telling him over and over again that I loved him more than anything else in the world. Those would be the last words he would hear as he drifted into the land of dreams.

Chapter 2
Don't Give Up

I remember looking over my left shoulder out of the large rear window of the limousine. My breath caught in my throat. I hadn't expected to see so many cars. Slowly, respectfully, they snaked around the curve at the end of the long somber street. Headlights on.

I didn't know there were so many people who cared. How did I not know that?

If only he had known how much he was loved. Perhaps he did know. Perhaps it just wasn't enough.

I don't remember much about those few days. It was as if I were living someone else's life. In someone else's body. Even as I look back now, there are distinct and specific moments I remember. And they follow a continuum. But it's the stuff in between that's gone.

In the early morning hours on Monday, July 25, 1988, I received a frantic call from my sister Kathleen. The ring jolted me out of a deep sleep. She was in London, Ontario, still living in the house that our mother owned. She shared the house with David.

Our mother, who at that time was spending the majority of the year on a little Caribbean island named Montserrat, had called Kathleen a few minutes prior. She was trying to reach David.

Apparently, Mom called him the night before but couldn't get through. So she thought she'd just try again that morning.

Kathleen went to rouse David so that he could take the call. After knocking on his bedroom door a few times with no answer, she let herself in.

There he was. Lying face up on his bed. Naked. Eyes open. Blood coming out of his mouth.

She rushed back to the phone to let our mother know what she found, and was immediately told to call me.

When I listened to Kathleen's voice, I thought there must have been some mistake. That somehow she just saw something else. I told her to go to the neighbor's house, and I hung up the phone.

A few minutes later, the phone rang again. She whispered, "He's dead." And I screamed.

Vaughn, a new tenant who was staying in the bedroom beside mine (I was living in my brother Denis's house in Toronto), came rushing into my room. I don't remember what I said to him. I don't remember any-thing I said or did.

Shortly thereafter, Bruce K., a longtime friend of De-nis's (and a friend of my family's), rang the doorbell. I opened the door to see his face heavy with grief, shock, and sadness. Unforgettable.

It must have been a couple of hours later when I was in my car, driving along the QEW highway, en route to London. I was frozen in shock. "Don't Give Up" started playing on the radio. And it was while I was listening to Kate Bush's ethereal, haunting voice that it hit me. When the reality of the situation could not be denied.

When I knew I would never see him again.

My dear, beautiful, sweet, sensitive, funny, intelligent, little brother David.

I don't remember anything that was said that day when I arrived in London. Surely phone calls were made. Arrangements were handled. But for the life of me, I can't remember a damn thing.

The only clear image I have is of my mother walking through the front door that night after her long and heartbroken journey home. I had never before seen her face look the way it did that night. I don't have the words to describe it. There was insurmountable sor-row emanating from her body. It halted her gait and weighed her down to such an extent that I thought she would never be able to lift her head again. I felt as though I not only lost my little brother, but that my mother was gone as well.

No memory of what was said or done. Until Thursday morning.

The limousine continued its crawl. We were almost at our destination. The Forest Lawn Cemetery was just another mile or so ahead.

I returned my gaze to the front of the procession. My eyes locked on the car that held the hearse where my little brother lay silent and dreamless.

As the wrought iron archway of the cemetery entrance passed above, I prayed that David's spirit was at peace. I hoped that somehow, somewhere he knew that he was loved.

September 2004

The National Suicide Prevention Lifeline receives approximately two million calls a year. Two million. And those are the people who choose to reach out for help.

How many countless others suffer in silence?

Why has suicide become such a pandemic in our society?

I hate to say this—I feel ashamed in doing so—but I am growing numb to the news of another life being tragically taken by someone's own hands. There are times when I must choose to numb my feelings, otherwise it's just too heartbreaking.

I cannot help but ask myself, sometimes out loud: What the fuck is going on?

Is it the crumbling of the family unit? How much does that play a part in the disappearance of hope for a fulfilling future?

Is it the secrecy, shame, and stigma that still exist about mental health issues, even though much progress has been made?

Is it because it's too damn easy to label someone as having mental health issues, when all it really is, is loneliness, and isolation, and fear of intimacy?

Is it just being fucked over too many times and giving up hope on humankind? Believing that no one is trustworthy?

Is it the lack of community that too many of us experience?

Is it our stupid smart phones and social media that oftentimes make us feel both connected and brutally disconnected from life and real human interaction?

Is it the pharmaceutical companies that offer so many drugs for depression and anxiety, and then peddle other drugs if the first drugs don't work? I love how part of the disclaimer for a lot of these antidepressants is, "May cause suicidal thoughts." Are they fucking kidding me??

We now know that a young mind isn't fully formed until around the age of twenty-four. And if that brain is under the influence of these drugs, it may not be able to handle the full side effects. David was twenty-one when he died from a pharmaceutical drug overdose. I still don't know who his psychiatrist was. Fucker.

Clearly, I have some anger issues to deal with.

Is suicide the last and only option when a tender heart is too broken to heal? Is that what happened with my David?

I don't have the answers. And try as I might, I will never know what was going through David's mind as the night of July 24, 1988, closed in.

But here's what I do know. I know that my family structure was never solid. And it began to unravel around the time of my father's death.

I know that living in isolation, even while (and maybe especially while) living under the same roof with many family members, destroys the soul.

I know that secrecy was rampant in my family. Still is.

I know that I get very scared as I walk around my city of New York, witnessing person after person hunched over, their eyes locked like a zombie's on their glowing screens. Unable or unwilling to peer up and risk looking around at what's happening right in front of them. Not taking the chance to look another human being in the eye.

It terrifies me when I see a two-year-old, four-year-old, ten-year-old glued to their phone or tablet while in a stroller or in a restaurant dining with their family. No social skills learned. No needing to learn how to behave respectfully in public, or how to gauge human behavior around them. Just placated and soothed by another world that gleams from their screens.

Talk about isolation.

I call it the new AA. Apple Anonymous.

But here's the thing: where there's life there's hope.

And the hope lies in knowing that I'm not alone in thinking this way. I'm not the only one who despairs over the lack of human connection that seems to be the new normal.

There's hope in knowing that there's more research, tests, and knowledge around pharmaceutical drugs and how they affect the mind.

I garner hope when I see people dining and having a conversation at a restaurant with no cell phones sitting on their table.

Hope rises when a smile is shared between me and a stranger as we pass each other on the street on a cool, crisp, sunny autumn day in NYC.

My heart is lifted with hope when precious time is spent with a close friend, as we muse over ways we can inspire more human connection through art.

And those two million people who reach out for help every year—I pray that every single one of them receives a seed of hope that will be planted deep in their hearts. Tended to. Nurtured and protected. So that in time, they will experience the strength in knowing that they belong here in this world. Come what may.

I hope they will know that they are already loved. Even though sometimes it feels like they aren't.

They aren't alone.

We aren't alone.

We are already loved.

National Suicide Prevention Lifeline: 1-800-273-8255

Chapter 3

Screaming

I am in Vancouver. Got here yesterday evening. It's now 9:45 on Thursday night. I was on the phone with my boyfriend about an hour ago. I called him from the restaurant where I was with my mother and my sisters. I had to call him because I felt like I was going out of my fucking mind.

It had been only twenty-four hours since I arrived, and I had completely lost my patience. "Sit down!" I barked at my mother when she got up to move closer to the hostess, who she thought was seating other people before us. She just can't let it be. She just can't trust anybody. She believes the world is against her. Everyone is against her. She's being slighted, mistreated, taken for granted everywhere and from everyone.

It's so damn confusing, this mix of compassion and anger. My heart breaks for her. I feel for her. She's been through some brutal stuff. And yet the rage that can emerge from me, like that moment in the restaurant, scares the shit out of me.

I want so desperately to just have a "normal" night out. I want to feel relaxed and not on edge. I want to know what it feels like to be in the world with my siblings and my mother and not feel like I have to watch the world out of the corner of my eye because no one can be trusted.

That's how I grew up. In a house built on an indestructible foundation of mistrust. Of everyone and everything. It's awful, because living that way means inevitably that a young, hope-filled vista of a promising life turns into a dark, solitary, small, windowless room. A spiritual, mental, and emotional prison.

It unfolds like this: You don't trust the world. Then you don't trust your community. Then your school. Then your neighbors and friends. Then your family. Then yourself. It's a slow metastasis that distorts one's thinking, erodes the heart, and strangles the spirit.

My boyfriend says that my mother's criticism and judgment are just external expressions of her inner anxiety and pain. He says, "She's not going to change. The situation is not going to change." He says he thinks it's tragic.

It *is* tragic. And on this day, the date of David's birth—and his funeral—the truth of that statement rings even louder and clearer.

I said to my boyfriend that I felt like I was fifteen again, when everything in me was screaming, "Get the fuck out!" Just to survive. Just to have some hope and possibility of a life.

Perhaps all that I need to remember now is that I am not fifteen anymore. That I do have a life. That I have created a full life as much as possible. That I'm not stuck here. I'll be in L.A. in four days.

The thing that breaks my heart the most though, is witnessing the ongoing closing off of life. Seeing how decades of fear, shame, and insecurity that are a direct result of mistrusting the world have warped my family members' perspectives.

It's such a curious thing, being with my family after having not lived in the same city for many years. I observe how the twisted familial behavioral loyalties still exist (a communion of depression, anger, lack of joy of life, lack of adventure, no friendships). And I simultaneously rake through my own life, looking at where and how I continue those toxic behaviors. They're not as potent as they used to be. But God knows it's a daily battle.

We were finally seated and awaited our meals. I started having a physical reaction to the negative experience. I felt slightly nauseous. And my third eye was spinning.

I don't remember what the conversation was about. But then one of my sisters started talking about having a lot of anger. I've seen that anger emerge at times, in spurts of vicious rage. It's no surprise. Suppressed emotions will inevitably be expressed one way or another. I asked her what she wants to do when she gets angry. She said, "I want to scream."

I tell her that I know the feeling. That sometimes it's good to just scream into a pillow, or even the mattress if the pillow isn't thick enough.

Ah, Dave. I understand why you needed to go. The guilt, shame, and anger that you carried around was too much. I hope you knew that even though I wasn't the best sister in the world, I loved you with all my heart. From day one.

My little brother. You are always in my heart.

July 28, 2005

The silence is the thing.

Surely there must have been times when we had great fun. There must have been moments when belly laughter was shared. But God help me, why can't I remember any? Barely any memories can be recollected before I was twelve years old. That was when my father died.

And then my teenage years...

We moved from Toronto to London, Ontario. At the time it was a city of around 300,000 people.

My mother was overwhelmed, understandably. Her husband had just died and she was left to raise five mixed-race children in an era and community where being mixed race was not considered cool. Not fucking close to being cool.

She sure did have to be strong. Frankly, I don't know how she did it. I can't even begin to imagine how difficult it must have been for her. All of it. God knows she did the best she could.

As I think back on those years, when I was twelve to seventeen—such vulnerable years of a young girl's life— my heart sinks. It was such a dark time. And I couldn't navigate through any of it. I stumbled, grasped, clawed my way through.

Imagine being a twelve-year-old girl. You move to a new city, your father dies, puberty hits, the family is fractured, no one in the house really talks to anyone else, the older siblings start leaving. It was awful. It was as though the move and the death of my father opened up a whole new chapter where loss and struggle prevailed.

The "n" word was thrown around by schoolmates. I was spit at once while walking to school by a couple of cruel boys. I had a girlfriend who lived across the street. Smart, funny, sweet girl. But things got complicated, and our friendship disintegrated. I don't remember the details now, but I felt saddened over the loss of our friendship.

I changed high schools three times. Never fit in. Never found a place where I felt safe and welcome. Sought solace and respite by having sex with the wrong boys. Was slut shamed. (Why is it that the guy is never shamed, but instead he is celebrated??)

By the grace of God, there was some inner drive that somehow made me keep going. Something that propelled me forward.

I moved out of the house when I was almost seventeen years old. David was around fifteen. The guilt I still feel to this day stems from that decision.

I left him. I abandoned him. My own fucked up need to try to survive, my need to get out, meant that I left him to fend for himself. I didn't even know it at the time. I don't remember even talking to him about it. Letting him know why I was leaving.

I don't remember what I was thinking or feeling around that time. All I knew was that I had to leave. Even if I did know how I felt, expressing feelings was not something that happened in my home.

I kept all my feelings to myself. We all did.

The silence. It was awful. When there's no outlet for a young soul to express feelings, then those stuffed emotions get twisted and distorted until they don't even seem real anymore. Until the notion of anything being real begins to dim.

I began to create and live in a world of fantasy. I would make up stories in my head about other people.

I distinctly remember riding in our car through neighborhoods, trying to catch a glimpse of other people inside their homes, always wondering what their lives were like. Fantasizing about who they were as a family, what they did together, how they celebrated birthdays and holidays. I would make up complete stories in a minute or less and move on to the next house.

Perhaps this behavior has been helpful to me as an actress and a singer. I am able to quickly conjure images that depict the emotion of the written word and then express them via my voice, whether spoken or sung.

But it sure isn't a helpful behavior when it comes to the real world. Especially when it comes to personal, intimate relationships. Oftentimes, to my own detriment, I have lived in a world of fantasy. Taken a kernel or seed of something and imagined it being more than what it was. Fleshed it out into a complete other world, filled with intimacy, love, trust. This has led to too many sleepless nights, kept awake by tears of confusion and despair.

Or, I have done the opposite. I have created mishaps when none existed. Needless to say, that's not conducive to creating or maintaining the most vital element of a healthy loving relationship: trust.

Do you know what I mean? Have you experienced the same thing?

Was there silence and secrecy in your home? Did they warp your sense of what was real and what wasn't?

Dammit. I swear. I'm crawling out of my skin right now.

I wish to God I could go back to that house at the age of seventeen, grab David's hand, look him straight in the eye and say, "I've got you," and take him with me.

Chapter 4

The Spirit World

The wail was trapped in my throat.

My head was thrown back and my mouth was wide open, stretched to its limit, trying to will the grief to finally free itself. But no sound came out. It stayed locked deep down.

The silent scream woke me up.

I had been dreaming of David. We were sitting at a picnic table somewhere outside. A place unknown to me, yet familiar. You know how that goes, when you're in a place that carries no memory from your waking world, yet in your dream it feels like you've been there countless times. I was sitting at the head of the table (if picnic tables can have that). My mother was sitting to my left. My sister Rose was at the far end of the table to my right. And beside her sat David. He was to my immediate right.

He was wearing a white shirt. I remember how he liked to wear white shirts. It made him look and feel like a young professional. Like he deserved to be respected.

Rose got up from the table and walked away as if she wanted to give us some privacy. Offer us some time alone to catch up. My mother stayed, sitting silently to my left.

David and I talked about unimportant stuff. Small talk. It felt so good to talk to him again and to hear his voice. I remember thinking while I was dreaming, while we were chatting, Wow, it's so wonderful to see him again! He sounded good. Just like I remembered. Thoughtful. Insightful. Funny. And he looked good too.

He was the timeless age of his death. Twenty-one. David had a beautiful face. Large and soulful eyes. A square jaw. A great smile. And his shoulders were broad. He was a masculine and handsome young man. I felt proud as I looked at him. Proud to be his sister. I was listening to him with my full attention.

And then something shifted.

As he was talking, an unsettling truth came over me. I began to realize that even though he looked and sounded alive, he wasn't. I could feel time slowing down, and I began to cling to his every word.

Then I heard my mother's voice. The only thing she said in the dream was spoken at this moment: "You know this isn't real." I glanced at her, but quickly returned my gaze to my little brother lest I miss another moment of being with him.

He changed in that flash of time. Gone were his eyes. In place of the sockets were two white lights. He was looking straight at me, and he reached out his left arm toward me, beckoning me to reach toward him.

But I withdrew. I didn't know if I was going to touch flesh or spirit, and it scared me.

Then all of a sudden, as if no time had passed, it all came flooding back. His death. The loss. The grief. And I could feel that grief gather itself and rise up within me. I opened my mouth to cry. And out came silence.

I've written before that if in a dream, or in that intangible but very real sliver of time that divides the waking and dreaming world, David asked me to go with him to see what it's like on the other side, I would go. I don't know if he was asking this time, but I can't help but feel like my impulse to withdraw from him was the wrong choice.

Remorse and regret haunt me. I feel like I missed out. Again. Just like in that dream I had years ago.

I fear that he will give up trying to reach me in the spirit/dream world. Please, Dave. Don't give up on me. Please try again.

September 29, 2010

Since the age of fifteen, I've kept journals. Most of them are in boxes, piled up in a storage space. I really need to decide what I want done with them when I'm gone from this earth. And I should probably do that soon. Not because I'm planning to leave any time soon (God willing).

But, well, you never know.

Every blue moon, I peruse through them. It's interesting to read my written words from long ago and recent times. Some things change at a rapid pace. Other themes seem to stay continuous and repetitive—clear signposts of healing that still needs to happen.

I wonder if certain wounds can ever heal.

I think about how I can sometimes be stuck in an immature and naive vortex of wishing and fantasizing that someday, somehow, everything will be "perfect."

It sounds silly. I know. When I become unmoored from reality and unwilling to accept what is happening right in front of me, stubbornly hanging on to a juvenile fantasy, I try to ease my grip as much as possible. That usually takes a conscious choice to breathe deeply into my pelvis, gently release my tongue that is no doubt stuck to the roof of my mouth, and visualize the energy that has created all things, surrounding me with healing light.

And then I feel centered again. Connected to Mother Earth, The Divine, and a part of the bigger rhythm of life.

Journaling helps a great deal as well. For you see, my mind can run about a thousand miles a minute, as it has been well muscled in the experience of fight-or-flight. I sometimes wonder if I am addicted to adrenaline. If survival mode has become too much of a way of life for me.

Maybe not so much as it was before. And it definitely was before. For decades.

But again, writing brings me to the present moment. Music does the same thing for me. No question about it. Particularly when I'm playing the piano and singing. The connection of the tangible (my fingers hitting the keyboard) with the ethereal (feelings expressed in the purest form via the voice) allows for countless stored feelings to emerge and release.

And dreaming—dreaming definitely is the portal of insight. And of hope and fear.

Amidst my journals (and too many voice memos on my iPhone recorded in the dark of night) are dozens and dozens of logged dreams. Hmm, maybe that will be a book for the future. Maybe I'll call it *Dreaming*. Or maybe I should think about that after I complete this book and the other book of essays I'm working on. (See what I mean about my active mind?)

When I dream of David or Denis, it's as if no time passes between that moment upon waking and realizing that the experience did not actually happen, and having seen them in the waking world so many years ago.

I know you know what I mean. It's such an unknown and magical thing. Dreaming.

I don't really ever want to know how it works or why it works. For it might be the last bastion of pure beauty and mystery that exists in this troubled world. As difficult as it may be sometimes. Dreaming is a world I love to be in.

You know, as I think about it, I imagine myself finishing out my days performing music, writing, acting (only in roles that are wonderful and thought-provoking), and dreaming.

Yes. I can see it in my mind's eye...

Having a little place in Italy with a view of hills and fields as far as the eye can see. Going there for a month or two at a time to write. Performing music around the world, just me at the piano. Acting in high-quality, intelligent projects.

And dreaming. Perhaps while nestled in the arms of a lover. Or just embraced in God's love. Dreaming.

Chapter 5
The Night Before

The night before David took his own life, I was out on a date with C.O. We had a lovely time. Passionate. Fun. A night that any young woman of twenty-four years would want to have.

I got home very late. I saw the light blinking on my answering machine. Yes, this was in the time when we had answering machines. Only one message. I played the message, but it was a hang-up. Someone called but did not leave a message.

Four hours later I got that call from my sister, who found David dead in his bedroom.

I knew then, and I know now, that it was David who had called me the night before. But I wasn't home. I wasn't there for him at the time when he needed me the most. I was out having a good time with a man.

Twenty-two years later, I was having a late night at a jazz club. I took my brother Denis there as a gift. He was visiting me in New York from his home in Vancouver, as he had done many times before. New York City and Brooklyn were the places he felt most at home, so he ventured there many times to see me, his father Roy, and Roy's wife, Merle. (Denis and I had the same mother. Roy was his biological father, who I had met many times along with Merle. Denis and I both called her Aunt Merle.) Denis and I had an incredible, memorable, joyful evening that night while watching a performance by the iconic Barbara Cook. Denis had asked if we could get tickets for her show while he was in NYC, as she was one of his favorite songstresses. I lassoed some tix and invited the love of my life to join us. At the dinner table prior to the show, Denis was to my left, and M was to my right. The two men I loved most in the world were right there with me. We were with each other.

Even though they met for the first time that night, they got along as if they had known each other their whole lives. I have never, even to this day, felt embraced and surrounded by love that was as pure and all-encompassing as I did that night.

It was, no question, the happiest night of my life.

The next day I saw Denis. I knew he had to venture back to Vancouver the following day, so I wanted to make sure that I saw him before his trip home. I was sleep-deprived. Happily so. I was in a state of bliss. Flying high from the night before, after having spent it listening to beautiful music that my brother enjoyed so very much, followed by romantic embraces with my love throughout the night.

While I was visiting Denis the next afternoon, I wasn't fully there for him. It was a brief visit. I was distracted by the possibility of a future with the man with whom I had spent the night. A man who was a true match for me intellectually, emotionally, sexually, and philosophically.

I wasn't there for my brother Denis, just as I was not there for my brother David. I was distracted by romantic fantasies both times.

It was the last time I saw Denis alive. And the love of my life chose another.

I haven't allowed myself to feel or experience sexual bliss anymore. I get close. But then I stop it in its tracks. A deep fear still resides within me. The fear that a night of romantic bliss will inevitably lead to a loss so deep that the temporary paradise is not worth it. And the dream of experiencing life with a soul mate vanishes in the blink of an eye.

July 10, 2016

As I read again the words you've just read, I'm struck with deep feelings of hopelessness.

And yet as I sit here in my apartment in NYC, gazing out the large corner window at the baby blue autumn sky and watching a flock of birds take flight in lyrical synchronization, I think about what my brothers would want for me. What they would want me to experience in my life.

I can feel them in the room with me right now. I swear. The space between the living and the dead has disappeared. And their spirits are here. Their love is palpable. They're holding me in their love.

Jesus. I can't stop crying. Grief and gratitude are so deeply enmeshed that all I can do in this moment is surrender. Just let it go.

It's so hard for me to do that. But I will try. One deep breath at a time. I will practice letting it go. That's the only choice I have, if I want to have a life for the rest of my life.

I know they want that for me. I know they want me to let go. Open up. Give myself a chance to experience romantic love again, come what may.

Love and loss don't necessarily have to be connected in my future as they have been in my past. It is time now for faith.

It is time now for me to allow the years of healing work I've painstakingly done manifest its goodness in my life.

It is time now for me to open. To risk. To love.

It is time now for me to step outside onto my balcony, breathe in some of the glorious, crisp fall air, look to the heavens, and daydream of love to come.

Chapter 6
David Saved My Life

The natural order of things leads one to believe that the older sibling protects the younger. It is indeed a sort of primal instinct. I sure know that I felt it long before I was old enough to even know what instinct was, or that it was even a word. You can see it in the aged photographs of Dave and me. You can see it in our smiles. In the way my eight-year-old arm is wrapped around his skinny little six-year-old shoulders. I can barely look at those photos anymore. The longing and pain are too great.

David's death was the catalyst for my move to Los Angeles. If he had not passed away, I would not have moved there. As much as the shock and disbelief of David's suicide still reside in my psyche today (after more than two decades have passed), knowing that if I had stayed in Canada I too would have died makes me continue to believe in destiny. Maybe my physical body would have stayed intact. But my spirit would have slowly died. No question about it.

Perhaps it was some kind of survival instinct that pushed me to flee, along with following the lead of my mother, who taught me that death means a transition. Not only from the physical world to the spirit world, but also from one place of residence to another.

My father, Cyril George Reuben, died when I was twelve. Shortly before his passing, while stomach cancer ate away at his broad-shouldered, tall frame, my mother chose to move all of us from Toronto to London, Ontario. I had never been there before. I definitely didn't want to pick up and move halfway through my first year of junior high. Even though I believe her intentions came from a protective and honorable place (it would be best for us kids if we moved from the big city of Toronto to a much smaller city), there is something inherent in my mother's nature that urges her to move frequently.

Since she emigrated to Toronto from Jamaica as a young woman, she has lived in countless properties. I have this nagging sense that since she began her life as a Canadian, she's been seeking a home. A real home.

I've never asked her about this. So perhaps I am projecting. Because I have experienced those same feelings and behavior.

I left home when I was barely seventeen. And I've moved so many times since then, it's hard to keep up.

But at that very tender age of seventeen, I basically ran. I needed to get out of there. I needed to find or try to create a home where there would be comfort, encouragement, unconditional love, joy, laughter, safety, and trust.

Ah, trust. The greatest missing element in my familial upbringing. Perhaps also the missing link in my mother's upbringing. Or did that begin after she moved to Canada? I will never know.

I watched and lived through my mother's slowly shrinking world, as the disappointments and emotional scars accrued over her life's difficult and complex journey led her to stop trusting people. Everyone either had an ulterior motive or was for one reason or another not to be trusted. So in turn, I had to learn the hard way about trusting people, both men and women. And these lessons were learned through trial and error.

I found myself trusting people who showed no reason to be trusted, but I did it anyway, trying to gauge my capability of trusting. Or I would walk away from ones who genuinely offered love, somehow not trusting that they were for real. Like an eager and hopeful child, I have run into the arms of men. Seeking comfort. Love. Safety. Trust.

I know that David was looking for it too. His soul was so open and loving, yet he didn't have the tools to help navigate his way through those unbelievably challenging teenage years in London, Ontario. A place and time when being a mixed-race family was like living as lepers. Challenges that were exacerbated by a family and a home devoid of connection, support, and trust.

The trouble is, when you are taught to trust no one, you begin to shut down. Because when it comes down to it, how do you trust yourself, or life, or God if you don't know what trust feels like?

I'm still learning about trust. I'm still learning about love. I may not have figured out the romantic part of love, but I do know about love between siblings. Between little brother and big sister. I know that sometimes nothing can ever fill the hole that is left after a sibling dies. It's a bond like no other.

And I know that by some Divine order, David is watching over me and guiding me from the heavens. As if he were the older sibling.

His death, the catalyst for me to flee a damaged young life, led me to a whole new world. He saved me.

October 1, 2010

My father was born December 1, 1890. Yeah, you read that right: 1890.

He was thirty-five years older than my mother. I very often ask myself, What did she find attractive? What was it about him that drew her to him? Why would she have sex with a man so much older than herself? Why would she have children with an old man?

Can you imagine how difficult it is for me to write about this? My heart is beating fast, and my mind is swirling with confusion, bitterness, and guilt. I feel guilty writing about the anger I feel toward him. And toward my mother.

Didn't they think about what the future would be like for five children to (inevitably) have to grow up without a father?

I sit here shaking my head.

My father had a "first" family. He had five grown children before he and my mother started having children. I met my half-siblings once. At my father's funeral. My mother didn't attend the funeral, because she felt so hated by them. So she sent us kids by ourselves.

Yeah, you read that right too.

(Denis, my mother's oldest child, who was born in Jamaica to the man who was my mother's true love, Roy, drove the car and took us to the funeral.)

Since I became a successful actress, I have heard from some of my half-siblings' offspring. And so the truth is, even though I have countless times said that I have no extended family, when it comes down to it, I do. It's just...I am in no way connected to them. And I'll be damned if I go ahead and "friend" them now just so they can say they have a celebrity in their family.

Fuck that. Where were they before I was on ER?

Oh, man. Do I have issues or what?

I've gotta ask the women reading this who were born into a family where their father was decades older than their mother: How do you feel? Was your father alive to see you graduate from high school? To even see you walk through the doors of your high school on the first day?

What's your relationship with him now, whether he's alive or dead? How did having an old man as a father shape your intimate relationships with men as you were growing up?

And for the men who are reading this, I've gotta ask you to do this: please think twice about having children when you're in your late sixties or seventies. Or even older. Really think about it. Because from where I sit, I find it to be an extremely selfish thing to do.

Not just the men who do it, but the women who choose to bear children for them.

When I walk down the street and I see a man with gray hair pushing a stroller, I automatically assume that it's his kid he's pushing. Not his grandchild. And a rage starts to simmer within.

I remember when I attended my godson's birthday party. He was turning seven. A man in his late sixties was there with his six-year-old son. The man was on his second marriage. He kept calling my godson's grandmother "Grandma," instead of by her first name. I had to bite my tongue. Had to. Because I wanted to jump on him the next time he snidely said, "Grandma," and say to him, "Hey, pal. You're old enough to be your kid's grandpa. So either call her by her name or shut your pie hole."

That probably wouldn't have gone over very well.

Perhaps you're thinking: Who the hell is she, telling people how to live their lives? Who does she think she is? How dare she?!

I couldn't agree with you more. I know what I've written is shitty on many levels. But I can't help it. I'm just trying to be as honest as possible about my own experiences. And my own deeply conflicted thoughts and emotions about this subject.

Obviously, if both of my parents hadn't been "selfish," then I wouldn't be here right now. So there's that.

But really, the deepest feeling I have about this whole thing is grief. And loss. And yes, a little jealousy.

It saddens me a great deal when I witness women, even women my age, who enjoy the company and love of their fathers. When my friends talk about their challenged relationships with their dads, I listen silently, wishing I had that very same challenge. When I see children playing in Central Park with their young fathers, my heart aches. And I walk away, immersed in my imagination.

Wondering what if.

What if I didn't have to learn at the very tender age of twelve the life-altering experience of the death of a parent?

What if I had a father who could have helped me navigate the extremely confusing terrain of my adolescent years?

What if I had a father who would stand up for me, saying with his eyes, "You'd better treat my daughter right," while in the presence of a young man who wanted to date me?

What if my father walked me down the aisle?

What if David had the presence and guidance of a father? Would he still be alive today?

I know how idealistic all of this seems. I know. There's never any promise of "happily ever after" just because someone has a father. We see all around us the decay of the family unit and the low rates of marriages that last, and in turn, families that stay intact.

I'm just saying that, for me, it's something I think about. A lot.

Maybe for the rest of my days, this is something that will always be a thorn stuck deeply in my heart.

I hope not.

Every day is a new start. Let me try again to ease the hurt and pain and slowly, gently remove that thorn out of my heart. For the last time.

Chapter 7
Major Geraci

'll never forget him.

Tall. Handsome. Athletic. With an open and warm-hearted smile, and intelligent eyes, full of soul.

As soon as he entered the auditorium, I was drawn to him. I sensed him before I saw him. There was something familiar about his energy. Yet we had never met so I couldn't quite place it.

Nonetheless, I watched him as he greeted friends and colleagues. And when he approached us actors who were sitting behind a table preparing to do a reading of a play, his handshake and steady gaze conveyed a depth of feeling and integrity that are rare in today's times.

We were at St. Vincent's Hospital Manhattan on November 9, 2009. It was a few days after the tragic shooting massacre at Fort Hood, Texas, where an Army psychiatrist shot thirteen people. And just two days before Veteran's Day. I joined the wonderful actors David

Strathairn, Jeffrey Wright, and Adam Driver to do a reading of the play *Theater of War*.

The play is based on a 2,500-year-old Greek drama that revolves around the personal ramifications of battle. How being at war affects the hearts, minds, and souls of not only those who participate in battle, but also the loved ones who deal with the mental illness, depression, and suicide that so often are the results from being at war too long.

Major Geraci sat in the front row, facing the stage, directly in my line of sight. I couldn't take my eyes off him. It was uncanny how much he reminded me of my brother David. Physically—his square jaw, height, breadth of shoulders, smile. The uniform—David was a cadet for a while. But also, there was something in his eyes. I couldn't put my finger on it. I just sensed a deep hurt brimming under the surface.

I turned to Jeffrey and whispered to him, "You see the soldier right in front of us? I don't know what it is... there's something about him. There's something going on with him...I don't know."

We read the play. It was overwhelming. The energy in the room was fraught with emotion. It was one of the most powerful moments I've ever experienced. Not just as an actor, but as a human being. The veterans, the loved ones, the new cadets, the mental health professionals—everyone in the room related to the story of the soldiers who were fighting hallucinations, rage, violence, isolation, and suicide.

After the reading, Major Geraci sat on a panel that consisted of him, a couple of mental health professionals, and another enlisted serviceman.

He was second to speak. He got up from the table and walked down the two steps that separated the stage from the audience. He wanted to talk to us as he would his class of cadets. Free of any constriction behind a desk. Close up.

He began.

He talked of how important it is for people who experience combat, either pre or post, to express their feelings. He used the analogy of a beach ball that someone might try to keep under the water, and he related that beach ball to an intense feeling. It's impossible to keep it submerged.

If you try to hold it down, it will pop up with a force that can hurt you, or anyone around you.

Then he spoke of his best friend from childhood, Tim, who was supposed to be teaching right alongside him at West Point. But Tim was killed in Afghanistan.

He started to cry. His tears dropped from his sweet face. More than a few times he had to stop mid-sentence and exhale slowly so that he could consciously take a breath. Let the beach ball float to the surface.

He spoke of feelings of loss, depression, and sadness. He spoke of trying to find meaning in a situation like the one he was going through. How sometimes he just couldn't make sense of it.

He spoke about how he was trying to use what he was going through to help other people.

He shared with us the story of how his wife, just a few months before, who was at that time seven months pregnant with their third child, suggested that they name their son after his dear friend.

I sat in the front row, in the seat he had inhabited just a few minutes earlier, silently sobbing.

He is the bravest person I have ever met.

I walked up to him as the evening was ending and asked if I could speak with him privately for a moment. We moved a few feet away from the others. I stood close to him and looked him straight in the eyes as I quietly told him, "You remind me so much of my little brother David, who passed away many years ago. He was tall, intelligent, sensitive, and handsome just like you are. Your cadets are lucky to have you. Your wife is lucky to have a husband like you. And your children are lucky to have a father who knows how to love. I'll never forget you."

February 2011

I have found throughout my life that nature is the place for me. The peace, colors, sounds (especially of wind blowing through trees), and balance calm me more than anything else.

Whether walking on the beach, silently sitting on a terrace that overlooks the rolling hills of Tuscany, hiking through the stillness of a mountaintop, or even gazing at the clouds that are nestled below while flying at 30,000 feet in the air, nature is my healing balm.

I'm very lucky to have a little place in nature that's a couple of hours outside of my mad, wonderful city of New York. This place is rented year-round, so whenever my schedule allows, and I feel my shoulders inch closer and closer to my earlobes, I hop on a bus and venture east. It's incredibly peaceful and quiet. Thank God. It's where everything seems to settle...my mind, soul, and heart rate.

It's where I'm writing these words now.

It's where I'm learning to trust. Gently. A little more each day.

It's not that I haven't trusted before. It's just that sometimes it only goes so far. I only allow myself to get close to a certain extent, and then I pull back. It's kind of a miracle, though, that I've allowed myself to trust as much as I have.

Needless to say, the flip side of trusting other people is trusting oneself. And that is a continuous practice for me, learning how to trust myself. Some days are easier than others. Some days I have to get back to the basics...

lots of water, rest, food, meditation/prayer, exercise. When I am able to do those things, I feel closer to my true self. Closer to The Divine.

"The Divine" is what I name the energy from where all things are created. I see Its mastery manifested in nature. And connecting to nature allows me to connect to myself.

I watch Its glory and power in the tempestuous ocean as a storm approaches from afar.

I hear Its magical music as the morning birds awaken me before dawn.

I smell Its fresh fragrance as I stroll through the quiet abandoned streets on a late October afternoon after a sweet rainfall.

And I feel Its hope and warmth as I witness the sun rising on a balmy July morn.

Yes, Mother Nature is the ultimate healer. And every day, if I stay in the present moment, my heart swells with gratitude to The Divine for guiding me here. For being with me as my heart gently opens and softens. For offering countless examples of trust. For nature is always there. Nature is constant. Supportive. Welcoming.

David and I playing and running through that field at our elementary school in Guildwood Village. The Divine is bringing me full circle. Remembering my time with my dear David as I once again find love and trust, in nature.

Chapter 8
"I'm OK"

I felt as though I was in a waking dream. Everything was so surreal. Things looked blurry and felt confusing.

Somehow I ended up standing solo, around six feet behind the rest of my immediate family. My mother, two brothers, and two sisters were huddled in front of the open coffin. I was, of course, a part of the family, yet very much a lone observer.

I couldn't see David's face as it silently lay on top of the cushioned interior. But that's OK. The image of his sweet face, forever now unmoving, was seared into my memory the day before when we had the viewing. Nor could I see my family's faces. All I could see were their backs, slightly hunched forward from the weight of sadness.

One of them suggested that we sing "Happy Birthday," since the day we buried David would have been his twenty-second birthday. (Somehow, amidst the planning, and scrambling, and tears shed in solitary privacy, it didn't occur to us that the day of his burial would be on his birthday.)

When I heard that, things became even more surreal. Like a waking nightmare. But then some sort of normalcy returned as someone suggested that maybe singing the birthday song wouldn't be a good idea. Thank God.

The room...I couldn't tell you what it looked like. I have no memory of the color, size, shape. I don't know what music was playing. I couldn't tell you what I was wearing, or what anyone else was wearing, or what the funeral director looked like.

But what I can tell you is, as I was standing there watching the scene unfold, locked in deep shock and grief, I heard David's voice.

No, that's not quite right. I didn't hear it in the traditional sense. I felt his voice. I swear to God. These words came from him and straight into my head and heart: "I'm OK, Glor. I'm OK."

He always called me Glor. The only person who has ever called me by that shortened version of my name. So I knew it was him.

My sweet, sensitive, beautiful little brother was consoling me from afar. After his spirit had left his body just a few short days earlier, his love was trying to help me. Guide me out of despair.

Jesus, I miss him.

I will forever be so immensely grateful for the time that he graced this earth and for the love he so generously gave. His birth...as a little girl, I felt like he was the best present ever. He was my little one.

I miss you beyond words, my little brother. Always will.

But I promise you, I will continue to heal. And grow. And as each day unfolds, I will practice forgiving myself. And I will open my heart again.

I'm OK, Dave. I'm OK.

July 10, 2018

55

David

1965. With my father
and mother.

Above: June 9, 1966. With my father and my brother Lennox. Guildwood Village, Ontario.

Below: 1967. David and me.

1969. Guildwood
Village, Ontario.

1967. Guildwood
Village, Ontario.

Above: Christmas 1972. Guildwod Village, Ontario.

Below: 1976. London, Ontario.

1984. David, me, and my brother Lennox. London, Ontario.

1984. London, Ontario.

Denis

Dad to the
left, Denis to
the right.

1972. Guildwood
Village, Ontario.

1986. At Denis's house. Toronto.

1987. Toronto.

1988. At Denis and Chris's house. Vancouver, B.C.

Above: 1988. Vancou-
ver, B.C.

Right: October 1988.
Leaving for L.A.
Vancouver.

Left: October 1988. Leaving for L.A. Vancouver.

Below: New Year's Eve 2004. NYC.

Left: 1996. Going to Emmy Awards. L.A.

Below: 1997.

1999. Wedding to Wayne Isaak. Port-land, Oregon.

2000. After Tina Turner
Concert. Toronto.

2006. Opening night of *Stuff Happens*. NYC.

September 8, 2010. The night of Barbara Cook's concert.
NYC. The last time I saw Denis was the next day.

DENIS ANTHONY LEOPOLD SIMPSON

NOVEMBER 4,1950 – OCTOBER 22,2010

Chapter 9

Dreaming

I love it when Denis visits me in a dream. There's often laughter in those dreams. And comfort. And unspoken guidance. Sometimes the dream can be so lucid, so tangible, that when I awake I can't help but cry.

It's such a distinct and mixed emotion, the joy of being able to see him again, look into his love-filled eyes, feel warmth and glee as I hear his voice and laugh, mixed with the sorrow that quickly emerges when I remember that I'll never see him again in person.

It has been five and a half years. That's a long time. Doesn't feel like it. And yet, as to be expected, a lot of things have happened during that time. A lot of changes. A lot of growth.

Yet still there's one area where I seem to be stuck in quicksand. Not quite being sucked under. Yet not being able to fully pull myself out. After all this time, I still haven't really accepted his death. I can't seem to accept the loss of his love.

I know that's fucked up. And I know people may look at my life from the outside and think it is amazing and easy. But it's not. Yes, there are aspects of my life that are filled with many blessings. I recognize them and am grateful for them, no question. I know how lucky I am to be able to live an artist's life. And I've certainly continued to expand and grow creatively as much as possible. But when it comes to my heart, I haven't done so well.

I have had quite a few gentleman callers over the last few years. (I say that with humbleness.) But even though there have been some lovely men, I've opted to say no to every one of them. I haven't allowed my heart to be open to any man. Can't do it. Won't do it.

You see, I just can't take the risk of losing again.

I know how childish and weak that sounds. Everyone knows that loss is a part of life. But my father died when I was twelve, my brother David died when I was twenty-four, and Denis died twenty-two years later. I never had the opportunity to say goodbye to any of them. So, I've had my fill.

Maybe I'm just making excuses. I don't know. Some days I can't see the whole thing clearly at all.

I have had relationships throughout my life, of course. But none stuck. I even got married. But I left the relationship. I won't go into the details of what happened and why. Just know, in brief, I have always left before I was left. Or I have chosen men who were not right for me.

Fear of commitment.

Yes.

Fear of intimacy.

Yes.

Don't worry. I'm working on this with a professional. Progress is being made. Because the truth of the matter is that I am yearning to meet a man whose love-filled eyes I can look into. Longing to be with a man whose voice and laugh will bring comfort and glee.

In the meantime, I'll wait to see Denis again. Perhaps I'll dream of him tonight.

April 4, 2016

Denis was fourteen years my senior, so he was already out of the house by the time I was five years old. Oh how I wish I asked him, when we were adults, about his perspective on the family life and his experience in our home. But I never did. I would often think, "We'll just talk about it next time I see him."

Please, don't ever wait to ask your loved ones the questions you've been longing to ask.

Our mother placed Denis in trusted hands in Jamaica when he was seven years old, as she left for Canada to begin a new life for herself and her son. My understanding is that when Denis arrived in Toronto, our mother was already with my father. I have tried to lasso more details from my mother about timelines and details, but perhaps some questions are better left unanswered. I really don't want or need to hear again the many ways my father let my mother down. These unsavory details will no doubt emerge if my mother starts talking about that part of her life. I'm not blaming or shaming her. I'm just saying...well, I think you get it. I just try to connect the dots as much as possible.

Here's what I do know: Denis spent many years under the roof where my parents mated, wed, and had children.

How did my Denis cope with that massive change of country, culture, familial dynamic? What was it like for him, this young skinny black kid from Jamaica, to be dropped into white Canadian suburbia? It must have been a great shock. Especially because the new head of the household was an old white man.

God, I wish we talked about that.

Thankfully, Denis had a great eye behind the camera, so the images he captured told a lot of the story. Many of the photographs of my parents, siblings, and me were taken by him. They're not kidding when they say a picture is worth a thousand words. There's one tiny photograph in particular that I keep framed on my bookshelf. I'm sitting on my father's lap on a wide Adirondack chair. I look to be around one year old. We're somewhere in nature. My mother is leaning against the chair where my father and I sit. She's smiling. She looks relaxed and content.

Denis captured another rare moment. My mother has a look of pure bliss on her face. Her head is thrown back, her eyes alit, and her smile wide and free. She is tossing David into the air. He's an infant. And he is also in bliss.

For the life of me, I can't find that photo. It's tucked away somewhere. I hope I can locate it, as I would like to see it again.

Denis. Thank God for him. He was an artist in every way. Singer, dancer, actor, director...and photographer.

The only rub is, since he was behind the camera so much of the time, it is a rare thing to have photographs of him with the rest of us. If only selfies existed at that time.

Denis was the light in our troubled world when I was growing up. Even though I rarely saw him, his visits (usually just a couple of times a year, as he was very busy and successful in the theater world) were the highlight of our days. Needless to say, my mother was over-the-moon happy when her firstborn would visit.

I don't remember many specific moments, just the feeling of his visits. It felt like the sun shining on my face after being sequestered in a cave for months.

There are just those kinds of souls, know what I mean? The alchemy in the room changes, brightens, whenever they are present.

He was that kind of light. And he shone it ever so brightly upon all. Including me.

When I was nineteen and moved from London, Ontario, back to Toronto, I stayed with Denis. My boyfriend at the time was going to move from London and join me. He did eventually. And then when my boyfriend and I parted ways, I lived with Denis for three years. That's when the osmosis began.

If he hadn't been there, if his heart wasn't as generous as it was, then I don't know what would have happened to me. Sure, I would have found my own apartment in Toronto and went on with things. But Denis is the one person who really believed in me and took me under his wing while I was a fledgling actress.

He kept me safe and warm under his gentle, sturdy, and steadfast presence. He allowed me to grow, strengthen, and blossom during those beautiful, joy-filled three years.

And when David died, Denis (who was by that time living in Vancouver) once again opened his heart and home to me. For you see, two months after David died is when I moved to Los Angeles, via Vancouver.

I packed up my little Nissan Pulsar and had it driven across country (a married couple wanted to take a road trip but didn't want to drive their own car). During that time I did an acting gig in Vancouver on the TV show *21 Jump Street* (starring Johnny Depp. Jesus, I'm old). My car arrived, I stayed at Denis and Chris's home (his longtime partner) and then I drove down to Los Angeles, never moving back to Canada again.

If it weren't for Denis, I can't even imagine where I'd be right now. Well, actually, I can imagine.

I imagine I would have stayed in Canada. Maybe continued acting, maybe not. But the acting thing isn't even important as I think about what might have happened internally. In my heart.

If I hadn't spent those three years living with Denis, I might never have experienced how life could be... filled with laughter, joy, friendship, community, support. Knowing that someone had my back, no matter what.

Since he's been gone, that has been the one element of life that I've missed the most. Knowing that someone's got my back.

There's a line from the movie *Gladiator* that rings so very true and describes my feeling about Denis, when I lived with him and beyond: "I've felt alone all my life, except with you."

Chapter 10
Nine Months Later

I was loved.

I didn't have to chase after it or question it. Denis loved me dearly.

I am sitting in my living room a day after hosting a wonderful Happy Birthday America party. I love bringing friends together. I love watching the joy and pleasure on their faces as we chat, nibble on yummy food, and drink lovely wine.

I'm thinking of Denis and seeing in my mind's eye how much fun he would have had if he were at my party, and how my friends would have loved him. His wit, humor, smile, spirit.

The TV is on but I'm not really watching it. I'm journeying through my imagination.

I had foot surgery a week ago, so I'm laid up at home for a little while. Unfortunately, the TV is on more than usual, but so be it. I hear the familiar voices of the cast of

Whose Line Is It Anyway? and I glance to the screen. Lo and behold, a skit has started about what an entertainer would do at a funeral.

My daydreaming has ceased, and the skit has my full attention. Try as I might, I can't bring myself to laugh, even though the comedians are hilarious.

For you see, it has all come rushing back. The image of my eighty-five-year-old mother standing at the head of the casket looking into her eldest son's face, quietly repeating his name. "Denis. Denis. Denis."

I'll never forget that image. And I'll never forget all that it took to make it through that time. From the moment I arrived in Toronto a few days earlier to standing there in Vancouver, five feet behind my mother, seeing her aged back stooping over, wishing more than anything that she could speak with her son again.

It was almost exactly the same memory and image that was cemented into my consciousness twenty-two years earlier, when I was standing about six feet behind my mother as she sobbed over the casket of my brother David.

I turn the TV off and put on some music.

I'm weeping. The music that just now happens to be playing on my cable channel is a piano piece that was part of the playlist I put together last fall. The playlist that was the only thing I listened to during those awful two weeks in Canada last October. The same reflective and sensitive solo piano piece that I would listen to first thing on those somber mornings. The piece that would gently ease me into restless slumber at night is playing now.

I am wracked with grief and loss. I realize how much I've been in denial about Denis's death. I have distracted myself with work or the pursuit of work. I have planned and hosted a July 4th party. I have placed my love and energy on men who are neither worthy of nor receptive to my affections. These efforts have been futile. There's nothing that can protect me from facing the heartbreaking fact that I will never see his face again. I will never again receive one of his bear hugs, or see his glorious smile.

Oh, my Denis. I love you dearly. I miss you.

July 5, 2011

How is it that grief knows no time? It's so confusing to me. Just over two decades pass since my little brother dies, and then another brother dies. And the space in between ceases to exist.

I'm no psychic but I am definitely very sensitive to the energy of those around me (hence my need to venture to nature to restore my mind and soul). One of my favorite pastimes is to sit at an outside café and people-watch. Mostly in small villages in Italy, when the majority of people's faces are not unnaturally bent over while staring at their phones. If you happen to catch the gaze of another, their eyes say it all.

Some have the wonder, adventure, lightness, and openness of a child. Some eyes look like they're on the prowl, seeking primal human connection. Others emit depth and pause. A wariness and hesitancy. As if they must gauge the intent of others before fully opening up and trusting.

Perhaps I'm projecting. More than likely I am. But if so, it's only because I desire to understand how we all deal with loss and grief. I want to connect with others who are as baffled by it as I am.

I want to know. I am curious. I wish I could ask you, How do you deal with it?

Is it relatively easy to shed a loss, knowing that you are securely wrapped within the thoughts and love of others who are still living? Do you retreat to heal and find that you've stayed in an emotional cave far too long, wanting to emerge but not really sure how to face life again? Or do you live somewhere in between, one day being in the world with an open and willing heart, the next feeling raw and unsure, only wanting the very basics of life—good hot coffee, nourishing food, water, and sleep—and mentally or verbally dismissing people who get in the way of those things? I cringe when I think about how much I do that. It's strange...the more vulnerable I feel, the more I can push people away.

Time and grief make no sense to me. And since I am a woman who wants far too often to make sense of things, I find myself pondering both things simultaneously.

I wonder how it's possible to throw a party nine months after a devastating loss and feel OK while doing so, but then a couple of hours later lose my shit.

I wonder how a song can boomerang me to a distant, distinct memory of the last conversation I had with my little brother, twenty-five years ago.

There is no logic to any of this. Do you know what I mean?

One way or another, I have just got to let it go. Otherwise, I'll spin myself into a mess.

Jesus, I need a boyfriend. Gotta release some of this energy.

Chapter 11
Shine

I was so overcome with gratitude that I stood there motionless, silent, with tears streaming down my face.

There were only three other people on the beach. Two had already strolled past me while taking their morning walk. The other was a solo journeyer like myself. He held what looked like a professional camera (the lens was so big I could see it from afar). He too awaited the sun.

It was a chilly yet unseasonably warm January morning. Two days into the fresh New Year. I woke up at 6 a.m., which is around the time I naturally wake up, and contemplated staying cozy in bed. Maybe catching a little more sleep. But then I checked a weather app and saw that the skies were going to be clear. So I got up, put on my fluffy red robe, wished I was kissing a new flame while he still slumbered (someone I'm interested in but have only kissed once), made some fresh coffee, and put on my warm socks, jeans, and so forth.

I got on my bike and rode the mile to the beach.

The sky was just beginning to lighten. I felt such pure joy, riding leisurely along the uninhabited streets at 6:50 in the morning. I can't explain it any other way than to say it was truly blissful. Nothing fancy. At all. Just the simplest beauty and peace, riding solo as the day began through small streets lined with old, lovely trees. Quaint houses with a light or two on. The larger mansions were empty of humans (as is often the case during the off-season by the ocean).

I arrived at my favorite beach and could hear the waves crashing gently as I nestled the front tire into the bike rack. When my feet touched the sand guiding me up the narrow pathway, my heart continued to open with gratitude.

The tide was low, and the sand along the waterline was compacted a little, so it was easy to stand. I stopped. Looked around. There was a thin layer of clouds along the horizon. Wispy. Billowy. Soft.

The moon was still high in the sky, looking delicate and grand. Assured of its place.

I walked a little, stopping many times to do a full 360 and marvel at the subtle shifting colors in the sky...light pink, rosier pink, blue pink, light purple, deep purple.

I wasn't quite sure where the sun would burst through the thin cloud layer until...until I saw one slice of it peek above the rim of Mother Earth.

I gasped.

The colors along the cloud line became bolder. More defined. Redder.

And then, like the opening of a tender heart when being embraced by love, there it was! The morning sun eased its way into the sky, cupped in a section of the clouds like a lover's hand cupping the face of his beloved.

It shone on my face. In all its glory. Welcoming me. Warming me. Loving me. I said out loud, "It's a miracle. It's a miracle." And it was.

It was a miracle that I was able to witness such a beautiful moment on the ocean, on the second day of the New Year, with a warm cozy apartment to return to. With an abundance of hope and love in my heart.

The tears came. And I let them flow. I thought of Denis. How he always told me to "Shine." How he beamed in a photograph where he was reaching up to the sun. And how I wished that he could be there with me at that moment, to witness such a glorious sight.

I stood there for a while and took it all in. Really took it all in. And I vowed to carry that light with me. To Shine. To be like the sun. Warm, loving, bright.

As I got on my bike to ride home, I couldn't help but smile. And smile big.

Writing this from my apartment in nature that has felt like home since the first moment I walked in, the same gorgeous sunlight is shining on my face as it streams through the second bedroom window, where my little desk is set up.

This is the happiest morning.

January 2, 2016

There really is nothing quite like a relationship between siblings. So much is learned about love. It's as if a whole other, deeper level of love is formed and happily leapt into. I think it's born out of instinct.

When I look at photos of David and me when we were toddlers, the feeling of love is so palpable in the images. It jumps right off the photo and lands in the heart. Looking at them can bring about an intensity that is unmatched. So sometimes I choose to not torture myself and take the easier route by just thinking of them.

There's still so much sorrow I feel over David's death. No doubt because it was so damn premature. And instigated and followed through by his own hand.

When I look at photographs of Denis, a different sentiment arises. Sadness, yes. Because I miss him so very much. But with the sadness is also gratitude.

Perhaps because my time with Denis, which really only started when I was around twenty years old, began a new chapter in my life.

Denis and I spent most of our time together laughing, singing, and enjoying many aspects of life's gifts. We were lucky that way. My too few years with David were much more daunting, as for the most part we (along with our other siblings) had to navigate through challenging times and emotional upheaval at home. David and I really never did get to experience many lengthy moments of fun or laughter. Not as far as I can remember anyway. Perhaps they are tucked so far back, stuck like taffy in the recesses of my mind, that I can't coerce them to join me today. Perhaps it's just too painful to try to remember. I honestly don't know.

Maybe I should try to find more photographs.

It's such a strange and curious thing when I think about my time with David and then with Denis. It's as if there were a Divine Plan that ensured that Denis and I would have the chance to build a foundation of a strong siblinghood (that we gleefully took part in), so that when David died, I wouldn't be left unmoored. Almost as if The Divine knew that I would have the most difficult of times after David died, since he and I were so close in age.

I'm not saying that my other siblings didn't suffer. God knows I am in no way implying that. All I'm saying is that Denis and I were simpatico. No doubt it had to do with the fact that we lived under the same roof for a while as adults before David died. And maybe it was partly because we were both entertainers (he was of course established already, and I was just finding my legs). But I suspect it is mostly because after David died, I was now the youngest living sibling, and Denis was the oldest. So as nature would have it, the oldest wants to look out for the youngest.

You know what? That's the very first time I've acknowledged that truth. Swear to God.

Wow. How did I not see that before? Maybe because Denis and I always felt so much closer in age than we were.

Now I see clearly how his beautiful and enduring devotion, protection, and support came forth instinctively as the eldest one. Perhaps subconsciously. And perhaps, just perhaps, he may have felt that since he wasn't really around for David's life (because he was sixteen years David's senior), he had somewhat of a second chance.

Maybe I was his second chance.

My God. Oh, Denis. Was that how you felt?

If so, I completely understand. For you see, Denis, you were *my* second chance. My second chance to be a devoted, protective, supportive sister.

My heart is bursting.

Chapter 12
Stick Man

"**M**ommy! Mommy! It's Stick Man! Hahahaha!!"
Denis and I would laugh our asses off
countless times as those words flew from
our mouths in high childlike voices. He was so darn
skinny. Not intentionally. That's just the way God made
him. Skinny as Stick Man. He would eat like a horse, but
it didn't matter. He would always eat healthily, which
of course didn't help. If we hadn't seen each other for
months, or perhaps a year, his skinniness would be the
first thing I'd comment on. I'd want to feed him burgers
and milkshakes. But alas, that never happened. He would
prefer a quinoa salad and a green juice. Hence the per-
petual skinny physique. Sometimes he would make the
sound of a xylophone as he plucked at his ribs. He was so
wonderfully silly that way!

He was quick to laugh and had bright eyes, a huge welcoming smile, and a generous spirit. Qualities that are perfect for a children's show. And that was exactly what he did many moons ago, for years. He hosted a very popular children's program in Canada called *Polka Dot Door*. He was so beloved and so recognized from his role that people would stop him on the street, in a restaurant, anywhere, and tell him that they used to watch him, and now their kids watched him on reruns. It was definitely a blessing and somewhat of a curse, as I'm sure any actor would understand. If you're highly recognized for one specific show or role, people will often reference it and want to talk about it, even though your résumé is pages long.

But Denis always handled it well. He was kind, funny, warm, compassionate, and always encouraging. He was human, though, and every human being has flaws. Of course, I can't really think of any that pertain to Denis. But God knows I have plenty.

I can be impatient, judgmental (especially of myself), and a perfectionist. I don't suffer fools well (I'm no Einstein, but I am pretty intelligent). I can be too quick to cut people off. I'm well aware of these negative traits and have been working diligently to eradicate them. Slowly but surely it's happening.

I wish Denis could see me now. I think he'd be proud of the progress I've made.

Amongst the many beautiful traits Denis had, one of them was graciousness. He was so very gracious to everyone. And that too was how God made him.

I learned a lot about being gracious, living with gratitude, seeing the positive, singing out loud at any given moment, being silly, laughing, being kind, and cherishing the ones you love from my sweet Denis.

He never knew this...I used to watch him on that children's show when I was a very young girl. Of course, he would visit a couple of times a year, but it was through the TV screen that I could see him, feel his presence, see his gangly, fluid body, hear his melodious voice, and watch that thousand-watt smile.

I'll never forget one late morning when I was sitting on the rug in my mother's bedroom watching Denis on the screen. I must have been around six years old. I remember watching Denis and missing him, since I hadn't seen him in quite a while. And yet there he was on the little screen. I remember a fleeting but intense feeling of, "I want to do that." It wasn't that I wanted to be an actor. I'm not one of those actors who say that they knew they wanted to be an actor since they were five years old. This was more of a desire to be able to connect with people the way Denis was connecting with me. Even though he was not there in person, I felt very emotionally tied to him as I watched him on TV. That's what I wanted to do.

So when I really think about it, it was Denis who un-knowingly planted the seed of inspiration for me to be an actor.

It wasn't until fourteen years later when that feeling evolved into me walking into my first acting class. It was right around that time when I moved into the house that Denis owned and lived in, in Toronto. And that's when I witnessed all of the wonderful qualities he had. That was the beginning of experiencing his loving soul in person on a day-to-day basis. That was the time when his gra-cious, gorgeous, generous spirit offered me the mind-al-tering opportunity to experience life in the opposite way of how I grew up. He led by example, through his friend-ships (there were many dinner parties that filled the house with laughter, conversation, and music), through his dedication to his craft, through his commitment to his career, and through the many hours of talking with me about life, love, acting, music.

Those were the happiest years of my life, those three years that I lived with him. Those far-too-brief three years before David died.

Denis was magic and grace personified. Skinny as he was, he had the heart of a giant.

September 11, 2016

What's your favorite comedy? Before you read any further, say out loud what your favorite comedy is and what your favorite line is.

Yeah, I know. I can be bossy sometimes.

Mine is *Revenge of the Pink Panther*. Inspector Clouseau (played by the unforgettable Peter Sellers) is such a polite Frenchman. He's also a little frisky. In one of my favorite scenes from that hilarious movie, he allows a beautiful woman to hop in his car, as it is late at night and she is stranded at a bus stop. Unbeknownst to him, she is actually a he. A short while later, the Inspector is held at gunpoint and forced to relinquish his car and his clothes. He has no choice but to swap clothes with his car companion. Surprisingly, the dress, "an original Dior," looks rather nice on him. As does the wig.

As an aside, I get that he would put on the dress so he doesn't freeze. But the wig too? Haha!

So...in the middle of the night, in the middle of nowhere, he frantically flags down a passing car. The car stops! Whew! Unfortunately for the Inspector, the car contains two police officers who mistake him for a lady of the night.

Clouseau tries to plead his case: "Don't let my legs fool you! I'm really a man!" *Hahaha!*

Sellers was such a master of fun ridiculousness. How did he (and his co-stars) keep a straight face while they were filming? I've seen that movie countless times, and I always laugh—sometimes so hard that I think I'm going to pee a little.

OK, another movie: Christopher Guest's *Waiting for Guffman*. The scene when they're doing the play for the New York agent (who sadly never shows up). The alien in the play "lands" and tries to walk through the space-craft's door, but its head is too big, so it bumps up against the doorframe. So deliciously stupid and silly! I'll never forget when my friend Laurie and I watched that movie and fell out!

Oh, it's such a blessing when two people share the same sense of humor. Life looks so much brighter and feels so much easier after a good belly laugh.

Oh man, Denis and I would laugh at the silliest things. We both possessed the same slapstick sense of humor, and if something ridiculous lassoed our attention, watch out. We could laugh till our bellies ached. Full throttle laughter. Ain't nothin' like it.

They say that laughter is the best medicine. They're not kidding.

Chapter 13
Opening

I read something the other day that has stuck with me. It was an article about a very well-known actor/director. One of those lengthy, in-depth pieces that's written to offer the reader an opportunity to get to know the person, not just the actor—and to hopefully garner big box-office sales on the opening weekend of his new blockbuster.

When he talked about his feelings of insecurity because of the relentless marathon of being on a hamster wheel in the television and film business (no matter how successful you are, you've gotta do and be more), I took notice.

The way he spoke about his panic and his anxiety to "get it perfect" very much resonated with me. I felt a little surprised, as I had always thought that this guy was one of the indispensable ones. The way he has always carried himself and presented himself in the world definitely conveyed that message. But when he quite candidly expressed how he often feels insecure in front of, or behind the camera, fearing that people won't like or respect his work, I felt for him. The simple honesty of his words revealed an endearing sensitivity. For you see, it's difficult as an artist to separate appreciation of your work from appreciation of you as a person.

I've been on this planet a long time. I know that we are all human. That we fundamentally share the same feelings and desires: to be loved, wanted, accepted, happy. And I certainly know that we are more apt to hide our fears and insecurities behind some kind of shield, whether we know we're doing it or not. Call it needing to survive in the world.

But this person took a risk and let his armor down. He laid the shield and sword on the ground. I felt such tenderness towards him and all humankind as I read that brief passage.

The fragility and delicateness of life are to be treasured.

As I sat by Denis's side during the last day of his life, the overwhelming loving tenderness I felt towards him—I've tucked it away a lot since that time. I have felt way too vulnerable to let others see it. Of course, there are a handful of dear friends with whom I can share my feelings. But when it comes to the ultimate vulnerability—loving again—I haven't taken the risk. I'm too fucking scared. Even though I am aching to be held, loved, seen, heard, and cherished, my lonely nights are easier to take than the possibility of loving and losing again.

But you know, I feel like maybe the time is coming for that to change. For me to change. For me to take that chance. And the more I stay open to the possibility, the closer I'll come to experiencing it. As unbearably naive and "Life 101" as this may sound, maybe all I need to do is want to open my heart. Maybe that's where I begin, with an innocent desire to try.

How wonderfully strange and unexpected. Just now, with the shift of intention, with the choosing to try, I feel the desire to gently lay down my shield and sword.

Maybe there's hope for me yet.

March 2016

If you were to line us up, my brothers, sisters, and me, from oldest to youngest, our skin colors would be: black, white, black, white, black, white. Sounds cool, right? Maybe in today's world it is. But it sure wasn't when I was growing up.

The issue of race has always been a very delicate and tricky topic in my family. Unfortunately, the message I learned as a child when things didn't turn out as my mother hoped, or if people were mean, was: they were that way because of the color of our skin.

That very well may have been true. Openness of mind around mixed race families was not a very common thing, particularly in the small towns of Guildwood Village and London, Ontario. But it doesn't mean that everyone did things "against" us because they were racist. That is neither a realistic nor a sane way of looking at, or living in, the world.

Yet I can only imagine how extremely difficult it must have been after Denis left the house and after my father died for my mother to raise five kids, all different gradations of black and white, in an era and in communities that weren't familiar with that scenario. It must have been painfully isolating and frustrating. I remember her telling me stories that when she would push my white siblings in a stroller down the street, some people who stopped and looked and then chatted with her thought she was the child's maid or nanny. Jesus. That must have been horrific and hurtful.

David had it tough. When we were in middle school and high school in London, he was called the "n" word. His skin was white. But his hair was curly. And of course, some of his siblings were brown-skinned. Sometimes when I think of that city, I feel such rage. I hated that place.

So yes, race and rejection played a large part in my formative years. And beyond.

Denis would tell me of his frustrations in the theater and television world. His thin frame, gentle demeanor, and Caribbean roots certainly didn't lend to him portraying a "tough black guy." So the roles he got were quite limited.

And for me, it was an immediate and brutal lesson when I moved to Los Angeles. It became very clear to me that I had to choose. Either I was black or white.

Obviously, my skin tone isn't white. So it wasn't that hard to figure it out.

But what was difficult was the response I'd get after certain auditions. A casting director literally said, "She's great, but she's not black enough." Many other times when receiving feedback, those words weren't said verbatim, but there was no question that that was the message.

Not black enough.

Denis...when he was a young boy, moving from Jamaica to white suburbia.

David...called the "n" word.

Me...neither white nor black in Hollywood.

It's very difficult, not knowing where you fit in. Always looking for that place. School, work, home. Times change. People evolve. Yet still, sometimes the pain of rejection lingers.

Chapter 14
Let It Rain

I t was raining that day as well. I had just checked into a downtown hotel, a few minutes from the hospital.

I pulled my luggage into the room, clicked on the overhead light, opened my iPad mini, turned on Stanton Lanier's album of tranquil solo piano, and opened the sheer drapes. It had begun to rain hard. And I stood there, looking down onto the streets of Toronto, frozen in confusion, shock, and grief.

Denis was a few blocks away, hooked up to life support. A massive brain hemorrhage the night before was wreaking havoc on his beautiful brain. It was flooded with blood. Swollen. Not working. Not alive.

Now, six years later, on the exact date that I arrived in Toronto and went straight to the hospital to see my dear sweet Denis attached to foreign machines that were breathing for him—his eyes closed, his gentle strong hands that were the only constant source of affection in my life unable to feel mine—I am astonished at how time can stand still. How trauma can freeze a person in a moment forever.

My heart broke and shattered into crystals that poured down straight into his heart. And that's where it still is. With him.

A psychic told me a few years back that he and I have had many lifetimes together. Sometimes I was the male and he was the female. Sometimes we were lovers. Sometimes only friends. But at one point we made a pact: whoever died first, the other would be there to take care of the necessary details. Apparently, according to this sage, in one life we both drank out of a poisoned cup instead of one of us being killed by a brutal ruler.

Yeah, I know how that sounds. God knows if any of that is true. I don't know. But what I do know is that I was and still am grateful to have been there with him, to take care of the details. And I know that I think of him every day. And I feel his presence, his love watching over me. And I love him so much for that. For accompanying me in the remainder of my days.

And I know that whether it is another six years, ten years, twenty years, or more that go by, Denis will always be the light of my life. Guiding me. Showing me the way. Loving me.

I miss him with every fiber of my being. And I pray that just as this rain cleans the air, trees, and streets, it will also freshen my spirit. Wash away the residue of grief that still encompasses my heart, and bring new life to my soul.

In honor of him.

October 21, 2016

The last time Denis was in my apartment was in September 2010, about a month before he died. I remember we were in my kitchen in the duplex I was renting on Twenty-Second Street in the Chelsea neighborhood. We were talking about my landlord's lack of boundaries and laughing about the madness of living in New York City.

He was sitting at the little marble dinette table, and my back was to him as I was slicing up some vegetables to put in the juicer. He was a very healthy eater, and I was doing my best to practice that behavior, especially in his presence, so making fresh green juice was a no-brainer.

Our usual banter had escalated to giggles, and we enjoyed the release from life's stresses. I remember thinking to myself, When he makes the move, when he finally decides to move to New York, that's when I'll adopt a child. Or maybe even have my own via sperm donor. We can be a family: me, my baby, and Uncle Denis. (Interesting isn't it? How the possibility of being in a lasting romantic relationship that would fill out that dream didn't even enter my mind.)

I didn't say those words out loud because I didn't want to pressure him. But I wish I did tell him what I was thinking.

Fuck.

Why didn't I tell him that I wanted him there with me? Why didn't I tell him?

Even though he had spoken many times about moving back to New York, I knew he was staying in Vancouver partly (or maybe mostly) because of our mother. She was elderly, and I think he was waiting. You know, waiting for her to pass before he moved. But then what happened? He died first.

Fuck. It's so fucked up.

Yeah, I'm dropping the F-bomb way too much, but at this moment I don't care. I swear to God, I was so pissed at her. Sounds crazy, right? But that's how I felt.

And a part of me was upset with Denis too. Why didn't he go after what he wanted?

OK, now I think I'm really losing it.

I want so much to blame someone. Because if I can place blame somewhere, then the whole thing will make sense. But therein lies the futility of it all. It will never make sense.

Some days I am on my knees, happily surrendering to The Divine's will and trusting in all that was and is.

And other days I am like a spoiled child who wants what she wants and is stomping her feet as she wails, "What about me?"

Today is one of those other days.

I feel confused, angry, heartbroken, and powerless all at the same time. Denis never moved back to New York. I never adopted (or had) a child.

I sit here with my head in my hands, realizing that once again it's time for me to surrender. Get on my knees, bow my head, open my heart, and ask for guidance.

There's nothing else to do.

Chapter 15
Denis On

Two days ago in Toronto, on November 5, while filming an exterior scene at a funeral home for an indie film, I glanced up at the street sign. It read, "LEOPOLD." Ah, Denis.

Leopold was one of his middle names: Denis Anthony Leopold Simpson. Such a regal name, wouldn't you agree?

His sixty-fifth birthday would have been the day before, on November 4. And there he was, showing me a sign of his presence. My heart was eased, as it had been an intensely difficult couple of weeks.

A trip to L.A., looking for new representation. Then Vancouver for a celebration party to honor five years since Denis left this planet. The next day, gathering at my mom's house for her ninetieth birthday. Traveling back to NYC only to depart thirty-six hours later for Toronto to work on the movie.

Almost as soon as my feet landed in Toronto, rage started spewing out of me everywhere. To everyone. For everything. At any given moment. Nothing was good enough. Everyone was stupid. Or an idiot. Canadians are too nice. Americans aren't nice enough. The project was below my standards. The coffee was too hot. People were driving too slowly. The hotel put me in a shitty room. There were too many loud talkers in the restaurant.

It went on and on. It got to the point where I didn't even recognize myself or my behavior. I was completely out of control. Terrified by the unmistakable feeling that I was running full-on to the edge of a cliff and no one was there to yell, "Stop!!"

Rage. Deep-seated fucking anger. My words tightly wrapped around red-hot arrows. And then, finally, I understood.

It surprised me to discover yet again how deeply enmeshed grief and rage can be.

I wasn't pissed off at the project, or the hotel, or Tim Horton's coffee. I was pissed that Denis wasn't there. I was enraged by the fact that I couldn't do a fucking thing about it. I couldn't help but believe that we should have been together in Toronto to celebrate his sixty-fifth birthday. Instead, I was standing outside of a funeral home on a brief break from filming, staring at a street sign, my tongue glued to the roof of my mouth and my breath stuck in my chest. I was standing in the city where, five years earlier, two weeks before his sixtieth birthday, I witnessed Denis take his last breath.

That's what all that rage was about. But you see, I couldn't tell anyone. Not while I was working. Because if I did, I would have lost my shit and cried for the whole day straight. And no amount of makeup would've been able to cover up my sadness. Rage was a lot easier to express. No risk of mascara running.

But alas, Denis came to the rescue. Once again. He was, in his way, there with me. His middle name printed out in bold. No one else noticed. No one else needed to.

LEOPOLD.

And then today...

I had finished a delicious pizza and a glass of wine after a very long workday yesterday. Went to bed at 4:30 this morning. Got up at around 11:00. Didn't bother to write or do yoga. Had to get outside. Breathe in some air. Do some things.

So I went to the bank. Then to a consignment clothing store. Then ventured to a new chic pizza place for a bite to eat.

While driving on Bathurst Street back to the hotel, I had a strong feeling. Like a pit in my gut. There was something about the street I was on that felt familiar. I glanced to my left as I approached the stoplight, and there was the hospital where Denis died. There it was.

As I made a left at the light, a beautiful rainbow arced across the stormy skies. I had to gasp at the timing of it. And the knowingness that Denis was once again showing me that he's with me.

And then, immediately afterwards, as I drove through another light (a light I'd driven through countless times when I used to live in Toronto), I glanced up. And there in bold print was the street sign, right above the street-light: DENISON.

DENIS ON.

Hi, Denis! I love you so much. So much. Thank you for your love that continues to bless and guide my life.

November 7, 2015

Nam Myoho Renge Kyo. Nam Myoho Renge Kyo. Nam Myoho Renge Kyo. Nam Myoho Renge Kyo.

That beautiful Buddhist chant. A devotion to enlightenment. To alignment with The Divine (or God, or Great Spirit, or The Universe, and the like).

I remember Denis practicing this chant. I did for a while as well. And I have recently picked it up again.

Denis and I (and my siblings) were raised Anglican. So we went to church on Sundays. I still love walking into churches, particularly ones in Italy that are hundreds of years old. Some have more positive vibes than others, that's for sure. But usually they can be a place for silent meditation. And for enjoying the magical union between man (the structure, the art, the music) and The Divine.

I have a small Bible that Denis used to carry with him. It was in his backpack—the one he had with him the day he died. I tucked the backpack away for almost six years after his death. Unable to open it and hold his possessions, pondering why he carried what he did.

Eventually, I asked a girlfriend of mine to sit with me while I slowly took out one item after another.

I thought it was a good sign that I was getting better at life, asking for help. My modus operandi has usually been: I can handle it myself. The trouble with that is people take you at your word. So understandably, they do indeed think that you can handle things yourself, even if the truth of the matter is that you are in desperate need of help.

In any case, this time around I knew that I wouldn't be able to do it alone. So she and I sat on my bedroom floor and I slowly, gently, and meticulously went through the pack. And there, amidst his hairbrush, keychain, socks, and store-bought eyeglasses, was this small, worn, brown leather Bible. It sits on my bedside table, still wrapped in the same rubber band, many pages earmarked, the spine broken and tattered, plenty of pages unattached.

It's one of my most prized possessions.

Prayer.

Meditation.

Chanting.

Nature.

Music.

Brother and sister.

Denis taught me through example how to practice connecting to The Divine. His love for me led the way.

And I can honestly say that through the years, those moments when I feel closest to Denis and to David as they exist in the spirit world are the moments when I envision the three of us enveloped in the iridescent, warm, golden glow of The Divine's love that holds us, and encourages us to stay connected to It no matter what happens.

Nam Myoho Renge Kyo.

Chapter 16
Pennies From Heaven

Denis!

Wow, brother, you sure know when I need you the most!

Today was my mother's birthday, and I gave her a call. I thought a couple of months ago that I would travel to where she lives to surprise her on her birthday. But I chose differently as the time drew nearer. Even though my last visit with her was a positive one, I couldn't take the risk that the next visit would be positive as well. There was no emotional consistency with my visits. And unfortunately, far too many of them were draining and taxing, leaving my heart swollen with confusion and sadness.

I am fatigued and stressed, and when I feel this way, I yearn for comfort, encouragement, understanding, and a shoulder to lean on. And I become like a child, wanting these things from my mother. But far too many times, it's me giving those things to her.

I love my mother. I do. And after so many decades, I still find myself struggling to accept the fact that no matter how much I give, on every level, her own wounds (that surely started long before I was born) can never be fully put aside so that her love for me, which I know resides within her heart, will fully be expressed. Free of any residue.

Some days I find myself thinking that one day a miracle will happen and we'll have the magical relationship I've always wanted. One where her love is unconditional. One where I don't have to prove my worth. Some days are better than others when it comes to learning that the emotionally mature thing to do is accept her and our relationship the way they are. But today was one of those days when I felt like I haven't learned a damn thing.

The call was a quick one. Her narcissism was in full swing, and I just couldn't take more than a few minutes. I was angry. Mostly at myself. Wondering when the fuck I'd grow up.

I got off the phone feeling resentful. Like life gave me the short end of the stick. But moments later I chuckled a little at my bad attitude, and I remembered the scene from the movie *Moonstruck* when Cher smacks Nic Cage across the face and says with intensity, "Snap out of it!" No need to ponder or fester in negativity. Just because my mother may have difficulty expressing her love, it doesn't mean that she doesn't love me. Also, it was a beautiful, crisp fall day in NYC, and I was about to meet my good friend Angie. She and I were going to another friend's place for a pumpkin-carving party, and then we were going to venture to my favorite little Italian restaurant. Perfect day!

I brushed off the hurtful feelings and hopped on the subway.

Maybe I've matured emotionally more than I give myself credit for.

I met Angie at my friend's place and showed her around the house. Just as we were about to climb the stairs from the basement to the kitchen, I thought of Denis. I spent the first Christmas after Denis died in that house. It's always a little bittersweet being there again.

A moment later, Angie stopped and pointed.

There, right by a laundry basket, was a shining penny. Denis!

When Denis was alive, he had this sweet habit: whenever he would see a penny he would pick it up. Didn't matter where he was or what he was doing. He'd say, "Lucky penny!" and he would scoop it up and rest it in his cupped hand.

There have been many, many moments since Denis died when I have glanced down and seen a penny, more often than not when I was going through duress. I might have been in a coffee shop. Or walking down a street in New York. Or at the airport. In the laundry room...anywhere. Denis would break through that thin veil between the spirit and physical world and would make a penny appear. Just for me!

Well, it turns out that he was also "contacting" Angie.

One day, about three years ago, Angie was at my apartment. We were having some wine and talking. She told me that she kept finding pennies everywhere, and she couldn't figure out what they meant. She had even called some family members asking if there was some significance to pennies. Angie's grandmother had passed and they were very close and also very spiritually connected. She thought maybe it was a sign from her grandmother.

As she was talking, my eyes bulged out of my head and my jaw slackened.

I got up from the sofa and brought over a small bowl filled with pennies that I had picked up and kept. And I told her about Denis.

We both couldn't believe it. And yet, we could not deny it. Denis!

There he was with us in my friend's house, saying, "Hello." He was there, on my mother's birthday, while I was with the one friend who has found countless pennies too!

We laughed. And I was grateful that my brother had lifted me out of a melancholic state of mind and into laughter. He did that so often. Still does.

Shortly thereafter, Angie and I walked a couple of blocks to a dive bar that was fully prepared for Halloween. It was a gothic kind of place with decorations to match. We talked of scary movies and I told her that I'm such a lightweight the video for Michael Jackson's "Thriller" still creeps me out. Haha!

We left the bar and strolled toward the Italian restaurant.

As we crossed East Fourth Street, I was telling her about the restaurant. She had never been, so I was excited to share my favorite food and wine with her. She had read an essay I wrote about Denis, and I mentioned that I wrote that particular essay one winter's day while sitting at the bar of the restaurant where we were headed.

Just as I said that, a car pulled up, the driver's side door opened, and "Thriller" was blasting so loud my hair almost blew back. WTF?! We laughed so loud and said, "Denis!"

You know, it's funny. As I'm writing this, I'm smiling. I'm no spring chicken anymore, and God knows how long I have left on this earth. But come what may, I know that everything is OK.

Everything is as it should be.

Lovers that have come and gone. Creative dreams that didn't come to fruition. My fractured family. It's all OK.

Denis reminds me of that, time and time again. All I need to do on those days when I am in despair is remember this beautiful fall day when I strolled through the magical streets of the West Village in NYC with a good friend, finding pennies and doing the "Thriller" dance.

October 28, 2018

I don't know about you, but one thing that has plagued me my whole life is the challenge of navigating my way through, and out of, familial loyalty. I wonder if it comes from a primal instinct since the beginning of man—the need to follow diligently the behaviors and beliefs of the parents. Maybe this needed to be done for survival. I think that must be the case.

But what happens as we evolve? What does one do if those behaviors and beliefs lead one down a path of emotional, psychological, or spiritual ruin?

Where can you draw the line? When does enough become enough?

I have struggled intently with this issue. By the grace of God, I have freed myself for the most part. I am learning to practice complete acceptance of the choices of behavior and beliefs that my family members have made. The only way for me to enjoy my own life is to live and let live.

Yet still, some days I feel that all too familiar tug. I feel guilty, shameful, and responsible. Those feelings were put upon me as a young child. Guilt, shame, responsibility. Somehow I was made to feel those things about almost everything. Jesus. It can be difficult to shake these ingrained, distorted beliefs. But I must continue to try to free myself.

I woke up this morning from a haunting dream...

My mother is walking down a hallway. She is her current age as I'm writing this. Ninety-three years old. She is walking on her own, but she often loses her balance and walks straight into the edge of a doorframe or against a wall, painfully bouncing off as she purposefully continues on her way.

I am witnessing this as I follow her from a few feet behind.

Hers is a stubborn gait. I can see people walking toward her with looks of compassion and concern on their faces. But she doesn't see or acknowledge them. She just continues down the hallway to a destination unknown to me.

I can see the side of her face. Her jaw is tight and clenched. Her eyes cold. I've seen this look before. Many times. It's a look that says, "Stay away from me. Don't talk to me." It's a look that bitterly displays an energy of aloneness. Like she can't trust the world. Or other people.

I'm watching the look on peoples' faces as they walk by. I sense that some want to stop and help her, but that look on her face—they dare not make a move.

My heart aches as I watch her. She is brittle. Frail, yet forceful. I know I am helpless. None of my siblings are there. It's just me, trying to keep up with her. Trying to prevent her from hurting herself.

She continues down the hallway. The dream ends.

I'm no master at deciphering the messages of dreams. But I sense that once again those feelings from long ago—guilt, shame, responsibility—have resurfaced. And that a part of me feels those things heavily as I tell the truth about my life. About what I remember from my upbringing.

The last thing I want to do is hurt my mother. But you know, this isn't about her. It really isn't.

This book, as painful as it is to write, is my truth. And that's what it's about. It's about telling the truth of my life.

I have lived far too long with silence, secrecy, and shame. Those things are killers. They are part of what killed my little brother. I must not be silent anymore. I must tell my truth.

No, this isn't about my mother. Actually, as I think about it, it's not even about me.

This book is about and for you.

I swear to God, if just one person who reads this book finds healing and hope, frees herself or himself from silence, secrecy, and shame, then each tear cried and every doubt delved into will be worth it.

As I lay in bed after waking from the dream, I practiced some deep breathing exercises to help calm my mind and reconnect me to The Divine.

Here's what happened: I felt a knowingness. My mind and heart were eased by The Divine reminding me that I can't save her.

I can't save her.

My mother is cradled in The Divine's loving care.

As I write these words, I am overcome by an overwhelming feeling of compassion, tenderness, and forgiveness toward my mother.

I can imagine, and yet I know it's impossible for me to fully grasp the depths of her pain. Her baby boy and her firstborn have died. All the dysfunction, silence, shame, guilt—all the things that plagued my formative years and those of my siblings—all I can do, all that's meant for me to do now, is to continue to express tenderness and forgiveness toward her. And toward my father.

That is where all of this has led.

That is where all roads lead.

To compassion. Tenderness. Forgiveness.

They did the best they could. Gave all they were able to give. Loved the only way they knew how.

That was, and always will be the truth.

Chapter 17

Going Home

I held him like the precious cargo that he was.

He was cradled in my left arm, and for the first time in my life, I felt how a mother would feel as she carried her infant in one arm and managed life with the other.

He weighed more than I expected. There were a few moments in the midst of trying to maneuver my way through the crowds at the Vancouver airport with him nestled between my left hip and shoulder when I thought, "I don't know if I can do this."

I wondered if some of the people who passed by knew what I was carrying, if there were others who had traveled on a plane with the ashes of their brother held close. I wondered if they could sense the grief that flowed through me, along with the great pride that swelled my heart.

I was so proud to be his sister. It was an honor.

I was fiercely protective of my brother Denis from the moment I got to the hospital in Toronto. I gave the nurse in the ICU a list of names of who was allowed to see him. After he died, I ensured that the viewing in Vancouver was for immediate family only, because Denis didn't want a funeral service. The guest list for the small gathering a couple of days later was constantly being shortened, as I only wanted those closest to Denis to come together so soon after his death.

And if the man who handled the details of the cremation got a little too personal in his comments about my brother, thinking it was OK to do so because he was familiar with Denis (as an actor), a look or a few choice words from me would carry the clear message: Be careful. You're treading on delicate ground.

This deep and ferocious protectiveness was new to me. There was no logic involved. I didn't think about what I was doing or saying. Actually, everything happened so quickly that there wasn't a moment to think clearly.

On October 20, 2010, I got a call in the middle of the night from Detective Adams in Toronto. He said that Denis had collapsed and was taken to Toronto Western Hospital. He was in a coma. He was on life support.

Four hours later I was on the first flight to Toronto, my hometown. It's funny how Toronto never really felt like home. New York feels like home to me. And Denis felt the same way.

He lived here many years ago, and he still loved New York. I had given him a little bit of a hard time the past few years, as he would repeatedly say that he felt at home here, especially in Brooklyn, and that he wanted to live here again. I would rib him and say, "Enough already with talking about it! Just do it!" We would laugh. And then when we would see each other again, him draped in his Malcolm X T-shirt, trying to look tough even though he weighed ninety-five pounds soaking wet, we would laugh again. He wore that T-shirt in the spirit of brother-hood that he felt in New York. He felt strong, confident, and safe here, yet I cautioned him about taking the sub-way too late at night. "You're too nice and too skinny!" I would say.

We both adored NYC, yet we were also proud to be Canadians. There was something about the politeness of my fellow Canadians that I so appreciated during those unbearably difficult two days in Toronto. The doctors, nurses, detectives—everyone was gracious, patient, kind, informed, and compassionate.

The head of the ICU told me with a steady voice and a clear, direct gaze that my brother had suffered a massive brain hemorrhage. That he would never wake up again. And that he was dying. I returned his gaze and said that I understood.

At that moment, something kicked in. A switch was flipped. A survival mode that I had learned decades ago took over. I functioned extremely well and coherently as I handled details, logistics, and planning. And it was during that week and a half, when everything seemed unreal and yet crystal clear, that I protected Denis with all my might.

I stayed at the hospital on that first and only night when Denis was there. I wanted to be close by. I curled up on the chair in his room, fading in and out of sleep. Then I sat close to him, and held his hand, and told him how much I loved him.

I felt blessed to be there. Alone with him.

A few days later in Vancouver, when my mother, brother, and sisters said their goodbyes to Denis, I was strangely content. I felt peaceful. Perhaps it was because I had slipped into the role of being the caretaker again. Perhaps it was because I had my alone time with him in Toronto. Or perhaps it was the discovery only two days earlier, of Denis's wish for his remains to be sprinkled in my garden. No matter the reason, during that hour I was at peace. And it was at that time when I fully understood why I was with Denis when his sweet spirit left his body in that quiet ICU room.

He wanted me with him so that I would be strong for our mother and siblings. I know that. In my bones.

There's something incredible about being by the side of a loved one as their soul leaves their body. I didn't want my desire for him to stay to impede the need for him to go. So I said with all the love in my being, "It's OK. Go in peace. Be at peace. I love you," while he took his last breaths. My heart broke, yet his was set free. And his freedom gave me strength.

So I carried him. To the airport. Through security. Through the immigration and customs areas. At times my glance fell to the ground in sorrow, yet all the while my head was held high, knowing that I was carrying precious cargo.

Knowing that he wanted to be with me.

Knowing that I was bringing him home.

June 2011

Afterword

The words written in this book emerged from a place of healing. Organically. Essay upon essay was written as a means for me to put into words the pain, grief, and loss I have experienced, as well as the joy, laughter, and light that have blessed my life. Putting pen to paper has always been healing for me.

The need to be an active part of my healing process was how this book began. And healing is its intent. I mean in no way any harm to anyone, whether family, friend, or foe. If what I've written has caused anyone any pain, forgive me.

Please know, please believe me when I say that I share my experiences with you from the depths of my heart. A heart that continues to learn about love. A heart that continues to grieve. A heart that seeks more joy in each day. A heart that continues to beat for healing.

Aunt Merle used to say, "Where there's life there's hope."

Indeed.

#AlwaysHope

About the Author

Gloria Reuben is an actress, singer, and new author. From her acting roles as Jeanie Boulet in the hit NBC series *ER*, Elizabeth Keckley in Steven Spielberg's *Lincoln*, and Krista Gordon in *Mr. Robot*; to being a backup singer for Tina Turner and then releasing three albums, Gloria's multilayered career has spanned decades.

Gloria is so very pleased to now be a published author. As her acting and music careers continue, so will her writing. Gloria is currently working on her next nonfiction book, an autobiography.

Gloria happily resides in New York City.